EVENINGS WHEN THE SUN

∂

John W. Schouten

FUTURECYCLE PRESS
www.futurecycle.org

Cover artwork, "Beautiful sunset over a duck pond" by Alaskajade with color treatment by Diane Kistner; author photo ©David Howells 2017; cover and interior book design by Diane Kistner; ITC Cushing text and Legacy Sans titling

Library of Congress Control Number: 2020953009

Published by FutureCycle Press
Athens, Georgia, USA

ISBN 978-1-952593-09-3

For my father, who gave me my love of words,
my mother, who gave me life,
and my dear wife Beth, who brings joy
to my life every single day.

Contents

Love Triangle with Neruda

Lines of Flight

Corvus Caurinus

I discovered only recently
a crow living inside me
Until then I had thought

the gnawing in my guts
was just black coffee
rolling into an empty stomach

It all comes together over coffee
The steam off the cup
echoes that which rises

from the rain-blackened street
where a crow
scavenges the pavement

Now I understand it
the heat upon the cold
interior surface, the breath

of a crow in January
How it all began seems clear
in retrospect

the egg of a dream I savored
in doubt and swallowed
Somewhere just below my ribs it hatched

Its hunger became my own
and it grew with the force of every light
I ever turned away from

Drum Song

The Spider Woman of Teotitlán

I will tell you how earth
in the hands of a woman
becomes water and then sky
and how she weaves
those strands of sky
into a history, a people, a dream

First she takes a chicken
or an armload of flowers
and barters for the wool of a ram
Matted with soil and excrement
it is a coil of Gaia's pubic hair

Next the river swells the fleece
a grey nimbus rising from the flow
and offered to the heavens
where it rains itself out and makes
its peace with the bleaching sun

The wheel of life turns
on a mahogany frame
planted in a swept dirt floor
Glossy hands twist pieces of the cloud
feed them to the wheel
and spin the threads of fate

Nothing bleeds like the cochineal
who lays her powdery eggs
in the pelvic curves of a nopal
then gives her life
to the alchemy of dye
In a wood-fired cauldron
the daughter of earth
boils the scarlet entrails of creation

Now it's time to dance with the dead
The loom and the warp
are the bones of her ancestors
Upon them she weaves births
and deaths, ears of corn
the flight of a hummingbird
The rhythm of generations
is the over-and-under path
of a wooden shuttle
worn smooth by the kiss of wool

The Dogs of Juxtlahuaca

The day they killed the dogs
in Juxtlahuaca we bought
big bags of hibiscus flowers
five-tailed comets streaking from the earth
to our hungry lips
color of blood, flavor of love

Surely they knew they were starving
the dogs of Juxtlahuaca
yet they wagged their tails in two-four time
as if angels
played their ribs like marimbas

Rivers of fruit swelled the village streets
A flotsam of mangos bumped
up against a raft of bananas
Fish, splayed and salted, schooled upstream
while flotillas of chilies
squared off with sides of aging beef

Market-day morning brought a feast
to the dogs of Juxtlahuaca
Town fathers in somber procession
heard confessions of hunger and served
a sacrament of strychnine and bread

A humble stomach wastes no gift
Soon to the music of barter and coins
the dogs of Juxtlahuaca danced convulsive jigs
took their bows
and retired to open-eyed sleep

Then hollowed out and light as air
they rose above the town
All the market hushed

We watched them circle, nose to tail
spiraling like smoke from a burning church
through a break in the clouds, and gone

Calcutta Taxi

The driver emboldened
by the whiteness of his fare
plays gas pedal, shifter and horn
like a video game he can crush
at this level with eyes half closed

He intuits the competition's nerve
by size of rig and quality of paint
sees gaps forming
before they form
shoots them like smoke through trees

I absorb the jolts and focus
on cows and kiosks
temples and mosques
prayer-flag laundry
strung along the street

When the flow clots long enough
for a shift to neutral the driver leans
out the door, ejects a stream
of betel-stained saliva, just like the spit
from khaki clad grasshoppers

I caught as a child
squeezing gently to reveal
the hidden colors of their wings
startling sapphires, scarlets and citrons
colors of Calcutta

where everything clashes
and nothing clashes and I arrive
at my non-destination
shoulder my bag and tip fifty rupees
to say thank you for the poem

I Dream of Lima

An empty beach
in the Peruvian winter and a woman
I hardly know
How we came here is a mystery

A flock of birds careens
in unison above the waves
wings flash silver
and I am alone

There lies across these dunes
a shanty-town
half a million souls
fallen on the sand like Andean rain

Drawn to the city by letters
from sons and brothers, they come
for the promise of work
and erase the road behind them

You meet them in the streets
the rich, furrowed earth of their faces
out of place
against the leaden Lima sky

In barrio La Victoria
a block from where I live and eat
a three-legged dog sleeps in a hollow
beneath a broken sidewalk

At night it forages
In the heat of day it lies
curled in shadows and peers
upward as people pass like clouds

Drum Song

The monk's head is shaven, serious
his brown eyes clear as polished pine
He squares his stance
grips the heavy sticks
and makes them dance across the temple drum
a thundering prayer
for the souls of earthly beasts

A thundering prayer for progress
rises from the hammers
and the pistons
and the clenched-fist crowds
of Seoul and Pusan
The turtle of long life is a picture in a book
The crane of happiness
lifts a steel beam skyward

Today in a grove at Kaya-san
I picked two ginkgo leaves
primordial fans from a tender branch
One I pressed
in the pages of this book
The other I set afloat
to ride the current
of a plunging mountain stream

Transplanting Season

Gather stones and soil
with a palette knife
Build a dike across a gentle slope
Level the ground
Flood the field with sky and clouds

Brush in shoots of new rice
short, vertical strokes
in two shades of green
dark at the heart
light where the air sifts through
For the egret, slender dragon
with rice-paper wings
add sweeping strokes of titanium white

Paint the sun low in the sky
a sign to start work or to stop
then sign the canvas
with a footprint, deep in mud
filled with brown water

As It So Unhappens

Crossing the campus alone
I look up at the clock on the campanile
It sags in its cradle of bricks
There's a chill, the tower
trembles, crashes to the ground

I remain calm
In the distance I hear a bus
gearing down

I search for meaning
in my body and find it
swept clean by the low-angling sun

Somewhere in a plane a woman
puts on lipstick
A car waits at the bottom
of the hill
Red

Runaway

A bus token jingles
against the nickels and dimes
in the pocket of his Pendleton coat
as he lingers at the door
of the Salvation Army
bookstore and wonders, if he enters
what new thing will happen to his soul?
Will it fold itself up like the city map
now lined more with creases
than with streets he's yet to search
for someone who might know her
who might have seen the face
that haunts him like a shadow of the one
reflected in the storefront glass
looking back with empty eyes
through words that spread
like ink across his brain?
All romance twenty-five cents

It's All Transformation

I like welding in a darkened shop
the frame in which all matter
and all that matters

are metal, fire and I
all experience reduced
to the silverskin of a perfect weld

Let us merge in flame
the scavenged parts
cast off from other lives

and rise, a scaffold
of precarious asymmetry
at its heart a stopped clock

and facing out
from a headlight shroud
a powerless iPhone fixed

to reflect the face
of every passerby that dares
to stop and look

Not Even a Close Race

My path to the 199th annual St John's Regatta
winds down through the Anglican cemetery
where stones announce dead people
Sleeping in the Arms of Jesus
or *Together Forever* and one
epitaph merely proclaims the stone itself
Erected by his Wife Beulah
with no pleasantries but duty fulfilled
in a most Anglican way and Beulah perhaps
glad to see the old sod off, and elsewhere
I recognize bouquets in festive plastic
from my trips to the Dollar Store
for bargains on dish soap and trash bags
and I wonder how my own epitaph
might be written on the wind
There flies the last of John X
who loved many, never well enough
and found better fortune than he deserved
And she who scatters the ashes may mouth
silently my final words: God, I miss you already

Political Winter

Gritty snow polices the landscape
scrubbing away color
like graffiti from a wall

The souls of the trees lie underground
drawing warmth only from the soil
In their branches crows

hunker down in dark cabals
withdraw into tatty coats and watch
as down below, hands

deep in pockets, and breath
escaping in thought balloons
walks the last free man

Geek

He preferred BVDs for their iconic
even generic recognition
but Hanes would do in a pinch, tighty-whities
were his only uniform
three packs of three every week
because three shows on Saturdays
and you could never get them clean enough
for a second show
He started a pot to boil
backstage because why waste
a good chicken? Annie who made
a mean chicken taco always
made sure the geek ate first and the Mexican
riggers prized her soup, cast lots
for the feet, sucked on them all evening
for luck or pluck, he wasn't sure
And the other thing he always did?
Bathed the chicken, tenderly
It started as a hygiene thing but became
a ritual of respect
for the live creature that gave its neck
to the spectacular bite and blood
to the pale skin and stark white briefs
and the ticket holders could never quite believe
how much there was or how it glistened
in the overheated air

Evenings When the Sun

Dead Horse Point

Blue fades to white where the sky ends
It is the same in every direction
The Colorado River suns itself like a snake a thousand feet below

From the mesa's edge I drop a stone
It bounces once, twice, then disappears
Its sound, too, is swallowed

In that part of my brain
that pertains to whitened sky
I understand, everything comes to this

Once I fueled my anger
with the history of this place: wild horses
driven to the mesa, culled, corralled, left to die

I nursed the irony of their deaths
by thirst
in plain view of the meandering river

I've tried to reconstruct God's language in the glistening bones
but their meaning escapes me
Visions of death move through me like wind through a church

The desert wells up in me
My legs grow heavy
Against the sky a solitary crow hangs crucified

Crosswinds

In the pale morning snowblasts
fly across the road
like rock salt from an old man's shotgun

Through the steering wheel I feel
their violence
Overturned trucks and trailers

litter the road like trashcans
Billboards hang splintered
road signs twisted and confused

Hollow cattle lie adrift
among derailed boxcars
as the AMTRAK glaciers by

Last night baking
in each other's heat we acted
as if nothing could touch us

oblivious to the clawing wind
to ghosts
writhing in the alleyway

Now I feel an urge to stop the car
to step into this landscape scourged by storm
but through it all I fear

I may pass untransformed
Where are you now?
Surely safe and warm

Rain Coming

The limbs of a sycamore flatten
out against this western sky
like the lines of a road map
There's a breeze
I can almost smell the distant
blackness, the rising Columbia River
At night sometimes it turns
on itself, runs backward
seeking its source
and the black-mouthed Chinook
ride it home
I've seen it from a car window
sailing down the Gorge
waves and debris
rolling gently upstream
silver backs lapping the surface
That dark eastward flow

Road Kills

This is the road I drive
a slick track
between the river and the wood
Night eyes shine at the roadside
Deer leap out of nowhere
Several times each winter
amber lights flash on the ice
as tow trucks brace
for tugs-of-war with the river

It's been months since I left you
lying in a wreck
of tangled words that cut
like iron and ice
Now you haunt the roadside
a movement in the trees
a face in the fog
You drift from the shadows
onto the road
I grip the wheel
My breath catches
You disappear

The other night
between my lights and those
of an oncoming car
a weasel sat bolt upright
on the center line
It froze
for a moment, blinded
then seemed to just lie down
The other car caught it

square across the back
and sent it arching upward
in a graceful back flip
Beautiful, I thought, so feminine

Evenings When the Sun

Evenings when the sun is broken
into layers of haze and smokestacks
waver like a mirage over the dark pond

when cattails explode to dusty rain
and settle on the silent nests
of marsh wrens

when squares of window light
emerge one at a time
from the darkening hillside

on evenings like this
I am the pond, the wren
and the dark places between the lights

Sleepless

A dog barks
Another answers
A car passes on the road and fades into night
The pallor of the streetlamp bleeds
through my window, yellows the blind
In the bedroom you stir beneath a single sheet
Starlings rise in waves from a mown wheat field
Trace them to a darkened page in the silence of this house

Observations at My Own Funeral

What is this place?
A sea wall?
People gathered at a pier?
I sense water here, and salt

Emotional contours shape the air
a granite fist lodged in ancient ice
the mineral smell of unfinished business
burrowing worms of fear

I begin to understand
This is not the shore
There is no boat, no cry of gulls
What I imagined to be floating here
is just a box of souring bones

My flesh and blood
are you also in this place?
Which of these huddled shapes are yours?
I sift through them and try to trace
your emotional signatures

Here a woman holds a picture
of me, only younger
and crueler
I get fraying paper, broken glass
sand at the heart of a misshapen pearl

And here a rage of muscle
a tongue-tied brain
a flash of sugar in flame
In him I hear my own voice
the bass line in a song
of hope, despair, disdain
My son, grow strong

And you
I would know you anywhere
You are my open country
I know every stream and every wood
Every blade of grass
I would inhabit, if I could
this empty space, this sparrow's nest
filling up with snow
I see you have kept secrets
Jewels wrapped in papery leaves
I will let them be
You have done as much for me

Small Things

i. The Tire Swing

From high in the maple
forgotten against the darkening snow
it hangs
a black
sleeping marsupial

ii. Matchbook

Matchbook said
to the beautiful woman
I would cut off a finger
to light your cigarette
To light your way
through a darkened house
or out of a moonless night
I would spend my life
flame by feeble flame
until used up and worthless
I was yours to throw away

iii. June Rain

The June rain
is so warm
it invites
participation

It cries
out
to be walked in

Shout!
it says
Run with me
down the mountain!

Snowy Egret

There's a woman I know
who walks
with the nervous grace
of an egret

To one side of her lies
a vanishing farm
an empty house
a fallow field

to the other, a river
cloudy with memories
steel doors
hospital corners

She stays alert
to ripples in the water
to rustling in the grass
And as she wades

in the muddy shoals
she keeps her dignity
but mostly she keeps
her distance

Staring at a Cheap Print of a Painting by Chagall

i. Stasis

A thread of thought lingers
between us like silk
It wants
some colored beads, it wants
a starry sky

I brought you flowers
a branch, really
The earth was in your eyes
Nothing would grow
I waited all night

Fields of mustard stretch
away over the hilltops
The air where it meets them
is stained with pollen
It drives the bees crazy

ii. The Village

Hand in hand these women dance
suspended from the clouds
The moon looks on, stars flow down
music rises from the ground

A deep sienna song
this furrowed field intones
that resonates with roof tiles
with our bedsprings and our bones

In this room two candles burn
Each from the other a shadow learns
of wick and wax but never of a flame
for light cannot block light

Crow

The crow exults in hawklike wings
takes to the sky on thermals
as if borne by the hand of God

yet not like the hawk to hunt
It prefers to take its meals
from gutters or fresh-seeded fields

Only to play does it take to wing
and if it sees upon the ground
some bauble or some glint of light

it spirals down
and with talons and beak
wrests pleasure from its find

The first sign of the apocalypse

is the green nose of a horsetail
pushing through the asphalt
at the edge of a road
This tender warhead stacked
atop its segmented missile
will not survive
the next passing tire, the next paving
but its plans remain intact
its manufacture indefatigable

Diana Reflects

On my skin I bear the scars of my creation
I am the yin and the yang
the burning and the forever black

At night the world is my dance floor
I pirouette, scatter light
trace orbits with my hands

When the sun comes up I suffer
become a ghost, a smudge of chalk
lucky if you see me at all

but tonight it matters nought
for while you stand there
heavy on the shore

I'll set across the water
and drive a silver shaft
deep into your core

Transfiguration

On our last night together you slept as if it weren't
Sometime past midnight, with the sand growing cold
I watched the tent of light propped up by the campfire sag
as another chunk of pine slumped into coals

I added a branch, blew a kiss and teased to life a new flame
that revealed upon the fire-washed sand a toad

Still and gray it sat in flickershadow
marking time with the pulsing of its throat
Breath for breath I matched its stillness with my own

A quick hop forward brought tightness to my lungs
With two more hops it closed the gap
to the ring of smoldering stones

Poised at the edge of the pit, now glowing almost white
it settled, sprang, and landed square among the flames

I reached for it and then recoiled
Beyond the point where flesh should char and skin curl
it sat unscathed, a tiny gargoyle
perched in the eaves of a burning church

It gave three languid blinks and left just as it came
with measured hops to stone, to sand
and to the night, once again a toad

Yarrow Stalks

Magazine-cover landscapes
blow by
in three-line titillations

A trigram of power lines
all yang all the time
define Heaven for a new I Ching

Lines on the highway
double yellow over broken white
hold fast against the wind

while breakers retreat across the beach
from windrows shimmering
with froth and radiation

and rows of rooflines
on suburban streets shelter
radiant daughters in swamps of desire

These are the signs of our divination
the lines we've drawn
a field sown with thunder

a stream in decline
the contrails of our dreams
in a gathering sky

Love Triangle with Neruda

The Superfluid Universe

Love is the dark matter
that flows from a furnace in the belly
pools at the feet, seeps

into the earth and warms
the seeds that someday spring
into forests of bone and blood

It is the storm
that flashes in the brain
lights up the eyes

and fills the unreactive night
like the dreams of a billion sleeping souls
blindly inhabiting the same space

Shadow Thief

I have a confession to make
It happened that afternoon
as we lounged in the company of clouds

The sun threw a few smoky rays
on our faces and your shadow
fell across my lap

With a blade of grass I cut
a sliver from that careless stain
and slipped it in my pocket

I've kept it all this time
In my darkest days I hold it

under my tongue
like a shard of broken glass

A Poem Writes Itself

The pleats of the drapery stand
back-lit by a restless sky
like the page ends

of a half-opened book
Your body, sleeping, seeks
my warmth

Black letters escape
like startled moths from the pages
of the book and light

at random on the bedsheet
instruments of beauty
and destruction

here on this page where knees
slide past knees, and ankles
intertwine in fragile

sentences, strands
spun from wings and woven
on a loom of moonlight and glass

Deleuze on Love

I crash into you crash into me
and the collision synaptic
and cellular splits
time into tangerine segments
and droplets so sweet they defy
gravity they define
possible they rip
giant holes in arguments
woven like fingers around fists
that try to contain
the expanding universe

Early Morning in Mapleton, Utah

It's cool, cold
        for June, the chill
wakes us, I put a quilt on the bed
we make love, you curl
into sleep
        At the window I hear
soft conversations, trees waking
Color bleeds into the valley
you turn
        breathe
deeply, and resettle, the canyon
walls are two cupped hands
filling with milk

Buttoning my coat I close
the door behind me, the canyon
breeze
        rolls off a slow
hill of rye. I cross the road, climb
the neighbor's gate and shake
hands with the tall
        grass
on the ditchbank, cows watch
with white faces
At a rise in the pasture
        I turn
to see the house, white, still
I think of you sleeping
Dew flashes
        on the grass, the back
of my neck grows warm
and suddenly, I feel planted

Sandpiper

From hardscrabble pine clinging to the cliff
head cocked just so
her entire form reflected
on the surface of his eye
Raven regards
the unselfconscious dancer
interpreting the music of the strand
where sand and sea and sky conspire to life
With drumhead brush and cymbal crash
and violins threading through
she makes
twenty-two pas couru
into the breaking wave, pulls up short
port de bras, one-two-three
point, dip, leap, retreat
Repeat
Raven admires
her slender legs, her perfect steps
her wildly beating heart
Imagines himself in pas de deux
in the salty fringe of depths
no raven ever knew
Imagines fashioning stilts
to extend his onyx stems
But his grace is more of mind than flesh
so he broods and gathers blooms
and plots to catch her backstage
where he will dazzle her
with his blackness and his wit

Bicycle Jihadist

With her smile
she infiltrates
my perimeter
Brakes squeak
Satchel swings
gentle with its load
fruit-scented grenades
aimed to explode
my heathen heart

Love Poem

Clouds break silver
on the mountains, and you
naked, pure light of dawn
flow over me
With one hand you open
my chest and plant
a stone
Black and smooth
it grows downward
into my soil, swelling
roots, and upward
crowding my ribs, filling
my lungs, it bursts
from my throat
a green, startling cry

Muse

In my mind there is a woman
colored California
with beach-glass eyes and seagrass hair

She rises over these languid dunes
like the moon upon the sea
and though her eyes are closed

they focus on some distant light
She parts her lips, her mouth

drinks joy, it is the source
and ending of the night

How I Miss You

I can't seem to stop this
hunger
You know how
cold my room gets
I woke last night
in a sweat
lit a candle
The flame just sank
in a pool of wax, turned blue
then black
I used to dream of you
Now I only dream
of having dreamt of you and woken

Love Triangle with Neruda

You on me rising
and falling while reading aloud
los versos más tristes
from a book split open
like an oyster on my chest

or a broken boat in the brilliant surf
el amor es tan corto
and I drowning with no memory
but your touch on my touch
tan largo es el olvido

the night is immense
yet you fill it with a breath
mi voz te busca en el viento
and of all the poems the saddest yet
is the goodbye left unsaid

Lines of Flight

Black Noise

In the belly of my hearing
a low-voltage whine
reminds me that I am
electrically charged
chemistry, and across
the room a ticking clock
last vestige of an analog world
plants fence posts
on which all other sounds entwine

What makes noise white
are random signals
within a tight emotional range
water in a stream bed
pulsing over rocks, sucking
at moss, eddying
in the arms of fallen trees
or a breeze
caressing a thousand trembling leaves

Then there are the darker sounds
the bass body blows
from a throbbing night club
the raw meat cough
the laboring of furnace and pipes
and all the anonymous cries
of a city that never shuts its eyes

What makes noise white is its ability
to disappear

What makes noise black is its ability
to pull us with it into the void

Seduction

i. The lie of the water

Come leave your clothes on the bank
and lead in with your toes

I will raise my silver mouth
as far as you will go

I will drink you
cool and clear

and still
there is no current here

ii. Surrender

Gather the sky
into ever tightening circles

Feed on globes of spent silver air
and disconnected syllables

Take me, hold me
bear me down

I breathe
a sweeter substance now

Coming Home in the Evening

Lightning rings the valley
lighting empty haylofts, stealing
the light from the trees
and after each flash I listen
for thunder
It doesn't come, except
as an afterthought
An uneasy breeze dusts
over the road, hisses
away through the grass and then
the house, the light
behind the drapes, the car
dark in the drive
You'll be on the couch
feet curled beneath you
a book in your lap or some
piece of handiwork
A train on the outbound track
There'll be others in the night
You'll sleep through them
but I'll hear: horns fading
boxcars rumbling away like dreams

Night Walk

It was nighttime in the back lot
My father, on one knee beside me
pointed to the sky
a blackboard with chalk stars
and strange shapes
He taught me
to find the hunter and his dog
the bear and her cub
and seven sisters of shining glass

Tonight I walk alone
through the quiet neighborhood
Winter comes
The trees rattle
By the streetlamp in front of my house
a shadow overtakes me
It walks on ahead, growing taller
I turn up the walk, the shadow
flows into the grass
and is lost like the stars at sunrise

My Father

My father rests in a cane chair
next to the pond he built
with his own hands
The smoke from his cigarette is carried
off by the sound of water
Floating on the surface a maple leaf
gathers light and paints
a broad hand on the cobblestone bottom
It's his hand
laying the stones
smoothing the mortar
priming the pump that draws
water, quietly, incessantly
to the top of the fall
where it trickles down stone
after stone in the mottled light
measuring the days of my father's life

Sorting

We move again
this time cross-country, so we spend
a day in the basement
deciding what to save, what to throw away

Certain things we keep
a cast iron skillet
some silver pieces from our wedding
wrapped in tissue

other things, old parkas
boots and the like go into a box
for Goodwill, it's little enough
Then I come to the deep stuff

Stuff from my youth
A microscope my father gave me
when I was six or seven
I keep for my own sons

now seven, five and three
I picture them marveling
at the same prepared slides I stared at as a child
wishing for one more step in magnification

one step closer to that secret world
Other things I do not pass down
A shoebox crammed with letters
from old girlfriends

I pull one out of its envelope
and start to read words that fade
to nothing in my hands, I imagine
the rest as blank sheets

folded neatly in their envelopes
I throw them away
And a box of black and white photos
one or two, a wheelbarrow

a gash in a tree, pique my imagination
Others have lost their meaning
I throw them away
One I find belongs to my mother

It is my father at nineteen
or twenty in a sailor's uniform
with thick, curly hair
and eyes that shine forty years later

like the eyes of a twenty-year-old
God he was handsome
Just yesterday we sat over Cokes
in an airport lounge, rattling the ice in our cups

as he described a weakness
they had found in his heart
He laughed it off and said
it would make the end come quick and painless

Still Life

The mahogany frame
of your mirror
bounds your rising breasts
a deep breath, caught
held, prelude to a sigh

Perhaps, if a painter
I could remake that moment
shattered by a footfall
a floorboard creak, and answer
questions that remain these years

The dusty half-light
a perfume bottle, a brush
And outside the window
the sparrows of winter
fat with dark berries and songless

What I see when I look through closed eyes because opening them hurts too much

Starlings swimming in a blood red sky
Aquarium windows
aquamarine to indigo
yearning for a passing fish

Amber burning in a garnet bowl
Spanish moss
dripping plums
into a pool of glass

Mirrors conversing in a dark wood
And a gray street corner
where you once stood
fussing with the collar of your raincoat

The Finest Flour

Somewhere on a mountain, you said
maybe at the roots of a big Doug fir
But I chose a giant hemlock instead
a few minutes' walk into the woods
The firs are majestic, but the hemlock
knows to bow its head

How tired and saggy we became
how loath to let an evening pass
without a bottle of wine and something
on the television, a foot in my lap
hungry to be rubbed, toes pulled
until they snapped

I regret the pangs of shame we shared
over all those hours of sameness
the hours of well-earned flab
slabbed off in hammocks of cool skin
the groans of laughter
at some darkly funny line

I've stopped watching, you know
The set sits dark and holding
half-watched seasons of HBO
and Showtime. The screen
projects an empty room
and glimpses of a passing ghost

I have a new habit
You might approve
I bake bread, a small loaf
every week on Sunday afternoon
By Thursday it's gone
I never share it with anyone

74

When I finally got the urn
I let it sit for the longest time
on the kitchen counter
next to the Mixmaster
that followed us around
the world and back again

In the fall I finally opened it
and sifted you
through a fine strainer
The coarser bits I took to the hemlock
That was a Sunday afternoon
By Thursday you were gone

The finest flour I transferred
to a crockery jar
I have two recipes I like best,
one that takes pumpkin seeds
and another with cherries and hazelnuts
To every loaf I add a pinch of delicate ash

When that is gone I'll bake no more
but I'll return to the hemlock
and ask it to compare notes
on nutritional value and flavor
knowing well before I do
I got the very best of you

Lines of Flight

Always disappear
Contrails disperse
as invisible crystals of gas
Rails and lanes converge

to points and then
to nothing, carrying steel
coaches like memories
into oblivion

A she-bear stands
in the trail ahead, considers
your relevance
dismisses you with a sniff

and a head-shake
and slips into the trees
just another stroke of black-to-gray
in a growing tangle of shade

Your lines of flight
your life lines and your love lines
were never more
than palmistry

that sleight of hand that leaves you
with two pairs when a full house
seemed not only imminent
but immanent

to a charmed life
and leaves you
with the simple realization
of randomness

That's the deal
no harm done, no hearts broken
and nowhere to go
but on

Acknowledgments

Versions of these poems have been published previously and are reprinted here with permission.

Calabash Cadencé Taisgeadan: "Geek," "The Superfluid Universe"
Canaries Coalmines Thunderstones: "A Poem Writes Itself,"
    "Love Poem," "Transfiguration"
Captiver Calliope Ten: "Not Even a Close Race"
Cardinal Cuento Tianda: "Bicycle Jihadist"
Caribou Coracle Terä: "Deleuze on Love," "It's All Transformation,"
    "Seduction"
Chickasaw Craft Threnody: "Black Noise," "Crosswinds,"
    "Lines of Flight"
Clarence Clobbers Tenderly: "Love Triangle with Neruda,"
    "What I see when I look through closed eyes because opening
    them hurts too much," "Yarrow Stalks"
Consumption, Markets & Culture: "As It So Unhappens,"
    "Corvus Caurinus," "Dead Horse Point," "How I Miss You,"
    "I Dream of Lima," "Runaway"
Coyotes Confessions Totems: "Evenings When the Sun," "Muse,"
    "Political winter," "Shadow Thief," "Sleepless" "Staring at
    a Cheap Print of a Painting by Chagall"
Cranberry Candlestick Terapi: "Calcutta Taxi," "Sandpiper"
Homecoming: Fishtrap Anthology Seven: "Diana Reflects"
Inscape: "Rain Coming"
Korea Journal: "Transplanting Season," "Drum Song"
Portland: "The First Sign of the Apocalypse"
Snakeskin: "Corvus Caurinus," "Shadow Thief"
Sunstone: "Early Morning in Mapleton, Utah" "Night Walk,"
    "My Father"
Verseweavers: "Road Kills"

The poems "Observations at My Own Funeral" and "The Finest Flour" appeared in *Death in a Consumer Culture,* ed. Susan Dobscha, Routledge, 2016.

"Crow," "Snowy Egret," "Still Life," and "Small Things" appeared in *Explorations in Consumer Culture,* ed. John F Sherry, Jr. and Eileen Fischer, NY, Routledge, 2009.

"The Dogs of Juxtlahuaca" and "The Spider Woman of Teotitlán" appeared in *Fire in the Pasture: Twenty-first Century Mormon Poets,* ed. Tyler Chadwick, Peculiar Pages, 2011.

"Sorting" appeared in *Highways and Buyways: Naturalistic Research from the Consumer Behavior Odyssey,* ed. Russell W. Belk, Provo, UT: Association for Consumer Research, 1991.

About FutureCycle Press

FutureCycle Press is dedicated to publishing lasting English-language poetry in both print-on-demand and Kindle (eBook) formats. Founded in 2007 by long-time independent editor/publishers and partners Diane Kistner and Robert S. King, the press incorporated as a nonprofit in 2012. A number of our editors are distinguished poets and writers in their own right, and we have been actively involved in the small press movement going back to the early seventies.

We award the FutureCycle Poetry Book Prize and honorarium annually for the best full-length volume of poetry we published that year. Introduced in 2013, proceeds from our Good Works projects are donated to charity. Our Selected Poems series highlights contemporary poets with a substantial body of work to their credit; with this series we strive to resurrect work that has had limited distribution and is now out of print.

We are dedicated to giving all of the authors we publish the care their work deserves, offering a catalog of the most diverse and distinguished work possible, and paying forward any earnings to fund more great books. All of our books are kept "alive" and available unless and until an author requests a title be taken out of print.

We've learned a few things about independent publishing over the years. We've also evolved a unique and resilient publishing model that allows us to focus mainly on vetting and preserving for posterity poetry collections of exceptional quality without becoming overwhelmed with bookkeeping and mailing, fundraising activities, or taxing editorial and production "bubbles." To find out more, come see us at www.futurecycle.org.

The FutureCycle Poetry Book Prize

All full-length volumes of poetry published by FutureCycle Press in a given calendar year are considered for the annual FutureCycle Poetry Book Prize. This allows us to consider each submission on its own merits, outside of the context of a traditional contest. Too, the judges see the finished book, which will have benefitted from the beautiful book design and strong editorial gloss we are famous for.

The book ranked the best in judging is announced as the prize-winner in the subsequent year. There is no fixed monetary award; instead, the winning poet receives an honorarium of 20% of the total net royalties from all poetry books and chapbooks the press sold online in the year the winning book was published. The winner is also accorded the honor of being on the panel of judges for the next year's competition; all judges receive copies of all contending books to keep for their personal library.

www.ingramcontent.com/pod-product-compliance
Lightning Source LLC
Chambersburg PA
CBHW070008100426
42741CB00012B/3154